Spirit Guides

A Complete Guide to Communicating with Spirit Guides and Guardian Angels

Jamie Parr

Table of Contents

Introduction 1

Chapter 1: What Are Spirit Guides and Guardian Angels? 4

Chapter 2: The Different Types of Spirit Guides 11

Chapter 3: The Purpose of Your Guides 16

Chapter 4: Why You Should Communicate with Your Guides. 19

Chapter 5: Defining the Terms of Your Relationship 28

Chapter 6: Staying Protected During Communication 32

Chapter 7: Communicating with Your Guides 42

Chapter 8: Talismans and Amulets for Your Guides 50

Chapter 9: Thanking Your Spirit Guides 56

Chapter 10: Getting the Most Out of Your Guides 58

Conclusion 63

Introduction

We are never truly alone in this life. Whether it be the fact that we are surrounded by billions of our own kind or the fact that we have an infinite number of different energies surrounding us at any given moment, we are never truly alone. Out of all that surrounds you, a handful of these energies are actually entities that exist to watch over you, guide you, and protect you in this lifetime. Whether you have a mission you want to embark on or simply want to enjoy a good day to day life, there are several beings that are helping you achieve exactly what you desire here on Earth. They are known as your *Spirit Guides*.

Spirit guides come in all shapes and sizes. Some appear as plain humans, while others are superhumans who possess unique qualities and strengths that are designed to protect and support you. Some are non-humans, taking on the form of angels, fairies, lightworkers, or even little balls of energy that have no real shape or distinct entity to them, beyond a familiar energy that you can recognize. Others still, take on the form of animals or mythical creatures designed to support you in whichever way you need. Regardless of what they look like, they all have one thing in common: you.

The spirit guides that surround you are known as disincarnates, meaning they have not incarnated on Earth, and they never will.

At least, not during your lifetime. In future lifetimes they may be the ones to incarnate while you are the one existing in their team of spirit guides, but in the meantime, their focus is on you. Spirit guides bring with them many wonderful attributes, ranging from the ability to protect and support you, to the ability to provide you with ample knowledge and guidance to help you achieve anything you desire on Earth. Some people believe we each come here with a unique mission, while others believe we come here with no mission at all and instead live freely with our own free will. Regardless of what you believe, you can rely on your team of spirit guides to assist you in your journey.

Even if you have not been regularly communicating with or connecting with your spirit guides, they exist and have been helping you in innumerable ways. Learning how to bridge the gap by opening the lines of communication will assist you in gaining even more from your spirit team, allowing you to tap into virtually limitless power that can be used to achieve anything you desire on Earth, and beyond. In the following chapters, you are going to discover how you can tap into your unseen spirit guidance team and call on them for safety and assistance anytime you need. As you discover how to tap into this powerful support team, you will find yourself experiencing far greater levels of success in all areas of your life, as well as deeper happiness and fulfillment in a multitude of ways.

The fact that you are here proves that your spirit guides are calling you to work with them in greater ways, and that you are ready to do so. If you are ready to embark on this exciting, loving mission and to experience life from an entirely new point of view, let's begin!

Chapter 1: What Are Spirit Guides and Guardian Angels?

Spirit guides and guardian angels feature only subtle differences between who and what they are, and why you have them in your life. Understanding these differences can help you know exactly who to call on in each moment, meaning you are more likely to tap into the exact power you need. To understand the difference between all of your guides and guardians, think of it like this: if you were facing an emergency because your house was on fire, you have the free will to call whatever emergency crew you desire. You could call an ambulance, a police officer, or even a tow truck if you wanted. However, none of these rescue teams would be equipped to help you with the emergency you were facing. If you were to call a firefighter, though, you would have the exact help you need. On Earth, you have the free will to call on the help of anyone you desire, though not all people will be able to help you. Likewise, you have the free will to call on the help of any spirit guide or guardian angel you desire, but not all will be equipped to help you. Knowing who to call, and when, ensures that you get the exact assistance you need.

Everything You Need to Know About Guardian Angels

The easiest way to understand what a guardian angel is, is to realize that they are a form of spirit guide. In other words, all guardian angels are spirit guides, but not all spirit guides are guardian angels. Guardian angels may be one of the most popular forms of spirit guides, as they are routinely talked about across various cultures and religions. Personal guardian angels may take on a lesser or common identity, or they may take on the identity of an archangel. If your guardian angel takes on a lesser or common identity, all this means is that the identity is significant to you and possibly a few others in your Earthly life, but no one else is likely to know who they are. For example, your grandmother could become your guardian angel after she passes away, which means she is a significant identity to you and your family, but the general public would not know who she was. Some people have archangels like Michael, Uriel, or Raphael as their guardian angels. Despite the fact that these may seem more prominent because they are "famous" angels, they are no more or less powerful than a lesser or common identity guardian angel. All guardian angels are powerful, special, and meaningful. You will receive the guardian angel that is best suited to you and your needs, which means that regardless of who your guardian angel is, they will have the exact power required to protect you and support you.

While some cultures believe that guardian angels are either those who passed before you or are famous archangels, others believe that guardian angels have no name and were not connected to you in any way in the physical realm. These individuals believe your guardian angel was assigned to you at birth and that you will never know who they are, but you can interact with them and communicate them. As far as spirituality goes, it is up to you to decide whether you will acknowledge a name and identity for your guardian angel, or if you will simply acknowledge their existence. Your guardian angel may not explicitly tell you their name, but you may sense who they are through the messages they deliver, and the energy they possess. If you choose to acknowledge a name and identity, you can use this as a way to commune with them. Of course, it is not necessary, and you can still confidently and effectively communicate with them even if they have no name or confirmed identity. It is all about what you are comfortable with and what feels right for you in this respect.

Your guardian angel is always near you, even if you do not sense their presence. In fact, they may intentionally hide their presence at times as a way to prevent you from becoming distracted or thinking too much about them when, in reality, they want you to think about and enjoy your physical life. In the angelic realm, not all angels are destined to become guardian angels; only some are.

For those who believe in Heaven or a higher realm that we ascend to following our death, guardian angels are said to guide you there. Through life, and through the process of your death, guardian angels can see the way for you to get to this higher realm and can help you make the right choices, as well as protect you on your journey there. In a way, they are sent to protect your soul from needlessly suffering by navigating you safely away from unwanted experiences. Your guardian angel will never abandon you, no matter what.

It is also important to understand that your guardian angel is a messenger. Whether you believe in God, the universe, or some other form of higher power, you can view your guardian angel as being the one that brings messages forth from that higher power so you can receive those messages. Guardian angels will provide messages through your dreams, your thoughts, and even through everyday life through signs, symbols, and other acts of serendipity.

You can communicate with your guardian angels in the same way you would communicate with any other spirit guide. If you wish for simple or casual discussion, you can speak to them within your mind or out loud as you go about your daily tasks, and they will hear you. If you wish to have a more direct conversation where you receive back-and-forth knowledge in that moment, you can meditate on them and ask to receive answers from them in that time. In this space, answers can come back through thoughts that "randomly" appear in your mind, as well as signs that may occur around you during that conversation. For example, some people notice that a butterfly suddenly floats by, a bird hovers outside their window for a moment, a candle flame goes out, or something else serendipitous occurs in their immediate space. These are all excellent signs that your guardian angel has communicated with you.

Everything You Need to Know About Spirit Guides

Spirit guides are much like guardian angels, except they are broader in scope. This means that spirit guides can manifest in far more forms than just as guardian angels. Spirit guides can be archangels or guardian angels, spirit animals, ascended masters, departed loved ones, or even energy forms that do not take on a specific shape or entity. There are likely many other types of spirit guides that you will experience in your lifetime, too, though it would be virtually impossible to summarize every entity in a single book, as there are infinite forms of entities that exist in the universe.

Like guardian angels, spirit guides exist to assist you through life and support you with experiencing whatever it is that you desire to experience on Earth. If you wish to manifest a specific thing in your life, spirit guides can help you do so by guiding you toward that which you desire, while also aligning everything in the energy realm for you to succeed. Spirit guides can bring forth specific knowledge, support you in your quests, and generally assist you in having a more enjoyable and fulfilling life.

It is often said that each human is born with a mission, and that your spirit guides are designed to help you achieve that mission. With that being said, on Earth we have free will, so we have the choice as to whether or not we want to identify and pursue our mission, or if we want to ignore our mission and simply experience life on Earth. For some people, the experience of living itself may truly be the purpose of their entire mission. Regardless, if you do wish to pursue your mission, no matter how big or seemingly impossible it may be, your spirit guides can help you to do so. They know the answers you don't, can draw forth the information you need, and can assist you in completing each step of your mission, no matter how challenging it may feel.

Like guardian angels, spirit guides typically will not communicate with you unless you first communicate with them. Still, they will always be around and will often help in ways that you had already agreed to, either at some point in the past or before you incarnated on Earth. They may help by pointing you in the right direction, miraculously saving you from a near death experience, or even providing you with the necessary insight to prevent you from pursuing a wrong path in life. For example, many people who have suffered from addictions or who have been living an unfulfilling life often report having sensed a "thing" that came to them and told them it was time to change, so they miraculously switched paths and achieved something grand. This is not an uncommon experience, and it happens to many people in many different walks of life. The result is that they achieve far more than they ever would have achieved had they remained on their previous life path, which was ultimately incapable of getting them the results they desired or needed.

Spirit guides may reveal their identity and entity, or they may remain unseen and secretive about who they actually are. Often, once you develop a relationship with your guides and the ability to communicate with them, you can ask them to reveal themselves, and they will happily do so, which actually helps deepen the bond you share with them. Even without this bond, your spirit guides will all help you. However, the bond often makes it easier for you to receive their support and trust in their guidance.

Your spirit guides can be contacted in the same way as your guardian angels. You can speak aloud to them or talk in your mind, or you can sit in a meditative state and welcome them to come to you and communicate with you in a more official way. They, too, may communicate with you through automatic or "random" thoughts, or they may communicate through signs, symbols, and serendipity. You will learn how to effectively communicate with your spirit guides later in this book, including how to converse with them and receive direct answers and guidance to any questions or needs you may have.

Chapter 2: The Different Types of Spirit Guides

There are many different types of spirit guides that exist. While we touched on a few of the basic entities in the previous chapter, there are actually five types of relationships you may share with your guides on a soul level. There may be more, but these five types of relationships are the most common and are the easiest to understand when you're first starting out. It is unlikely that you will need to know about or understand any further types of relationships, though your spirit guides will always lead you to more answers should the need ever arise.

The five types of relationships with your spirit guides you are likely to experience include ancestors, soul mates, soul families, twin flames, and soul assigned guides. Each one relates to you in a different way and, therefore, plays a different role in your life, just as different relationships in your physical life serve different purposes, with people who play different roles, too.

Ancestors as Spirit Guides

One of the most powerful forms of guides on your spirit guide team are ancestors. Ancestors are people who were biologically related to you on Earth, and who carry a great connection to you and your soul, as well as a unique understanding of your life experience. Regardless of what your relationships with your living family are like, your ancestors will always love and support you unconditionally as they wish to see you, and your shared lineage, succeed in your soul missions.

It is important to understand that ancestors will maintain the same personality and level of abilities in the afterlife as they did on Earth. While they will continue to learn and grow; often growing past many of their more toxic traits, they will still have the same personalities and abilities as they did on Earth. For example, if your great aunt loved gardening and hated technology, she would be a wonderful spirit guide to call on when you need help gardening, but not the right guide to call on when you need help with a digital concern. You may not always be aware of what your ancestors are good at, but you can always find out by asking them and being open to receiving guidance and answers in any form in which they may come.

Soul Mates

Soul mates are a specific type of soul connection that are destined to cross paths with you. Many of your soul mates are Earth-side and can support you like a spirit guide. However, they are not the type of spirit guide you can call on at any time like a guardian angel or a disincarnated ancestor. Soul mates are linked to you in a special way, often behaving like eternal best friends, though occasionally having different types of relationships with you, too. Some soul mates share a specific type of intimacy with you and will express that intimacy either in this life, or before you actually incarnate.

It is important to understand that soul mates in your spirit guide team are different from the types of soul mates that are often talked about in romance novels. Unlike the star-crossed lovers version of a soul mate, spirit guide soul mates are souls that are linked together through a form of eternal connection, though they are not required to be physically present in each other's lives for any period of time. In fact, they may never manifest in this lifetime at all.

Soul Families

Soul families are similar to soul mates in nature, though they have a more imminent bond. Soul families tend to find their way into each other's lives in every single incarnation, regardless of which incarnation it may be. Your soul family will present itself on Earth by appearing in your life through close familial connections or friendships, which become so close that they seem like family. They will also exist in your spirit guide team, representing beings and energies in other realms that are an obvious part of your family, too.

Soul families often share a similar mission, usually to avenge familial karma on one level or another and will work together to achieve their missions. Whether you realize it or not, on a practical and energetic level, you and your family will always be working toward something similar in your personal lives, as well as in your relationships. The idea is that you all work together to empower each other's missions and create success within your family unit.

Twin Flames

Twin flames are guides who are very similar to you and that have a very strong spiritual connection with you. They serve to help you both on Earth in physical endeavors, as well as in spiritual endeavors.

Your twin flame is said to be the same as you in virtually every way, meaning they have a unique understanding of who you are, how you work, and how they can help you through specific missions. When you two work together, whether it be on Earth or in the spiritual realm, you create the opportunity for you both to experience great success in your Earthly and soul missions. The power you create together is massive, and it is nearly unparalleled by any other power on Earth or in the universe. Connecting and working with your twin flame, either in the spiritual realm or on Earth, is an incredibly powerful way to help you both live to your ultimate potential.

Soul Assigned Guides

Soul assigned guides are like guardian angels, spirit animals, and other entities that are assigned to you from birth. They may not have any sort of specific connection to you or your soul, but they do have a unique reason for being present on your team of spirit guides and helping you toward your specific mission. Often, your soul assigned guides have a similar mission as you, will gain something from your mission as well, or have a karmic debt they need to repay and are doing so by being your guide. Regardless of why they have been assigned, their purpose is to be a part of your spirit guide team and to help you achieve success on your soul's mission, whatever that may be.

Chapter 3: The Purpose of Your Guides

Understanding the purpose of your guides helps you feel more confident in calling on them and trusting that they will actually be there to support you. Each guide has their own unique reason for being in your life, though they all serve a wonderful purpose. It is important that you understand the purpose of your guides so you can call on them when needed and know, for certain, that they will help you.

Support Us in Our Soul Missions

Some guides are with you for the purpose of supporting your soul mission. They may have the same mission as you, or they may even be the ones that encouraged you to accept a specific mission in life. For this reason, they stay with you as a way to help you fulfill your soul mission, as they can provide you with guidance and helpful information you otherwise would have gone without. Guides sent to support you on your soul mission will give you information on how to fulfill your soul mission and provide insight into what action to take. They will often align universal energy to ensure that the "stars align" in your favor, which further helps you to achieve your soul mission.

Guide Us Through Universal Energy

Your guide may be assigned to you as a way to help you navigate universal energies. Some guides will accept this as their mission, similar to how people on Earth feel deeply called to do something like work as a doctor to save lives, or work as a lawyer to help innocent people be absolved of criminal charges. Once a guide has accepted this as their mission, they may be assigned to you so they can fulfill their purpose. Following the assignment, they work with you to help you navigate through universal energy. These guides act as a sort of universal mentor, helping you with your soul mission or any new mission you may create for yourself. They are wonderful to work with as they have no personal agenda or desire to help you in a specific way, meaning their guidance is totally unbiased and open to helping you fulfill whatever you desire to do with your life and free will. These guides are wonderful for personal missions, manifesting, energy work and energy healing, and other quests that may be entirely separate from your soul mission or karmic work.

Assist Us in Reaching Mutual Goals

Sometimes, a spirit guide may have a similar goal as you do, so they team up with you to achieve that mutual goal. Similar to how business partners will work together to achieve a mutual professional goal, spirit guides may team up with you because they have similar karmic debts to settle, or they have a similar energetic mission as you do. By teaming up with you, they are able to receive the benefits of your Earthly incarnation, much like how you receive the benefits of their disincarnation. As a result, you are both able to work toward your mutual goals and help each other succeed.

Allow Us to Avenge Our Karmic Debts

Many people believe that each of us has a karmic score or balance that we hold in our spiritual lives. Karma must always reach a neutral balance before we can officially reach the end of our karmic journeys. Some of us carry negative karma, so we are incarnated on Earth as an opportunity to avenge our karmic debts. Spirit guides such as our ancestors, soul families, and other guides will often work with us to help us avenge these debts, so we can officially reach a zero balance and end our karmic debt cycle. This way, we are in neutral karma and able to be free of the suffering associated with carrying a negative karmic balance.

Chapter 4: Why You Should Communicate with Your Guides

Even if you agreed upon a specific soul mission before incarnating on Earth, you are never obligated to communicate with your spirit guides or even work toward your soul mission. Upon coming to Earth, we do so with one single clause in our soul contracts: we ultimately get to decide. Some people incarnate on Earth with a specific mission, only to realize that their ability to fulfill that mission is impeded by something, or they realize there are other things they would rather do while they are here. Many never even think to ask themselves why they are here on Earth, and what their unique purpose is. Our free will gives us the choice to either fulfill our soul mission or to ignore it entirely.

Making the choice to work with your spirit guides, whether it be to fulfill your mission or to simply get to know them and leverage their guidance in other ways, is a highly personal choice. You are never obligated to do this. However, there are many impeccable benefits you can gain from engaging in this type of work.

One thing worth noting is the occurrence of mediums and other spiritually attuned individuals who are capable of identifying and introducing you to your spirit guides. These types of sessions are a wonderful way to become connected to your spirit guides in a way that feels comfortable for you, particularly if you feel safe with the mentor that is guiding you. However, it is important that you also learn how to communicate with your guides on your own, as this ensures that you can communicate with them and receive their guidance without requiring a third party to help you. This makes receiving and following their guidance far easier, allowing you to gain the maximum benefit possible from your relationships with your spirit guides.

Deepens Your Self-Confidence

Learning how to communicate with spirit guides has been known for helping people drastically deepen their sense of self-confidence. This comes from three specific areas of benefit that you gain from communicating with your guides: confidence that it is truly them you are talking to, confidence in the symbols you receive, and confidence in the fact that you are deeply supported in life.

When you have a third-party individual facilitate communication between yourself and your spirit guides, there is always room for a level of skepticism or uncertainty to exist. You might wonder if it is truly your guides that have been contacted, if what the person is telling you is true, or if they adequately interpreted the messages being sent by your guides. Readers and interpreters will always have their own unique way of interpreting messages, which means what they say may be slightly off from what was intended, and in your intuition, you will know and feel that. The issue here is not that you have received a poor reading, but that you were not the one personally identifying the messages that were being sent to *you*. Often, the messages are highly personal, and only you will know how to properly interpret them. Learning to communicate with your guides will help you receive and interpret your own messages, so you have absolute confidence in the messages you are receiving.

The confidence you gain from the symbols you receive enables you to have clearer, more effective communication with your spirit guides. This means that rather than having broken or uncertain communication, you lose the language barrier and are able to clearly understand exactly what your guides are telling you. You will begin to see their signs more often and notice them clearly. Confidence in your communication leads to confidence in your action, which means you are far more likely to gain your desired results from your communications.

Lastly, you gain confidence from the fact that you are deeply supported and always feel guided in life. One of the many reasons we lack confidence is because we experience fear, and fear is often felt when we do not know what is coming next. When you realize that you have guides supporting you through the unknown, it becomes easier for you to move through the unknown with confidence because you know you have someone always looking out for you.

Increases Your Personal Faith

Having faith in something that you have not personally interacted with is challenging. You may believe that something is true and that it exists, but it is hard to personally have faith in something that you are yet to see or experience in your own way. Creating personal interaction with your spirit guides means that you receive signs, symbols, and messages from them directly, which makes having faith in them far easier. The deeper your faith in your spirit guides, the deeper your ability to trust in them and receive their guidance.

The deepened faith ultimately comes from communicating with your guides and experiencing undeniable acts of serendipity or signs of something unexplainable occurring. For example, if you ask for a sign from your guide and look up at the clock only to realize it is 11:11, you know your guide is right there. Or, if you ask for a highly specific sign such as to see a yellow bird, and within a few minutes you see one, you know you have received a sign from your guide.

Receiving signs from your guide is an incredible experience that is challenging to explain, and difficult to justify or describe in any way other than serendipity or the presence of a higher power. These types of signs can rarely be described as coincidence because they happen so frequently and in such a way that it is hard to deny the fact that there is a direct link between your communication and these experiences. As a result, you know in the depth of your heart that you are receiving true signs and being supported by your unseen spirit guides. With this direct personal experience, you know that you can call on your guides and rely on help as needed.

Improves Your Strength and Power

Each of us has the capacity to tap into incredible strength and power, both within ourselves and within our spiritual energy. In order to tap into your spiritual energies, you need to be able to actually believe in them and understand how they work, as well as communicate with them with certainty. Learning how to communicate with your spirit guides ensures that you are not only tapped into that power, but that you have mentors who understand the power you have tapped into and who can guide you on how to use it. Again, many spiritual mentors and coaches exist on Earth who can guide you toward using energy and deepening your connection, and their services are often phenomenal. However, nothing compares to the personalized guidance that comes from working with a team who knows you more intimately and thoroughly than anyone else does, or even can in the first place. Regardless of how powerful a medium or reader may be, they will always read with a level of bias that makes the reading slightly more personal to them than it is to you. Again, this does not mean they are not good at what they do; it just means they are reading with a typical human bias that every human on Earth has.

Once you understand what your guides are saying, you can implement it in the exact way you have been guided to do. Since it matches your direct power and abilities, you create the opportunity to enjoy a stronger relationship with your personal energetic powers. If you wish to open your third eye, activate your clair senses, or engage in activities like astral projection, having the support of your guides makes for a far more successful and empowering experience. You can learn more about how to awaken your third eye and work with your clair senses in my book *Third Eye Awakening,* and you can learn more about astral projection in my book *Astral Projection.*

Another great benefit of working with your spirit guides is that if you want to develop a new ability or discover what other hidden energetic or spiritual talents you have, your spirit guides can help illuminate this. They can see you in a way that no human can, which means they can quickly and easily identify certain abilities you might have that you can use to your advantage. Once your guides have helped illuminate said talents, they can also help you understand them and use them to the best of your ability, while adding their own power to grant you even greater extrasensory abilities.

Creates a Sense of Meaning for Your Life

Going about your life without any connection to the spiritual forces that exist to support you can lead to a life that always seems to be missing something. You may not be able to identify what, specifically, is missing, but you can feel that something is. Often, people who experience this sense of something being missing find that they do not seem to be living up to their potential, that their dreams are going unmet, or that they are struggling to even create dreams in the first place. Rather than living a fulfilling, invigorating life, they live a life that seems bland and boring. Essentially, they exist as a part of the mundane majority, rather than tapping into the phenomenal world around them so that they can engage in magnificent experiences.

When you learn to communicate with your spirit guides, they can use your intuition to guide you toward your soul mission, or toward creating a new mission for yourself, which you can then pursue with their assistance. As you pursue this mission and experience success in your efforts, you find yourself creating freedom in your life and attracting a more excitable and enjoyable reality. When you have this energy at your disposal and have awakened to all that exists around you, you begin to truly understand how wonderfully magnificent life can be.

Helps You Experience Deeper Fulfilment

The mundane majority that have yet to awaken to the depths of reality believe that fulfillment can be gained by pursuing any old goal and fulfilling it. In their minds, all you have to do is pick something and go for it. Their method for creating fulfillment seems highly random and often fails to take into account the unique nuances that make each of us special. While this may seem to work for them, those of us who have been awakened on any level will discover that this method for achieving fulfillment is predominantly baseless.

You have a specific yearning within that you desire to fulfill, and every urge you experience has attempted to push you toward fulfilling that yearning. Whether you intend to or not, you are wired to discover and fulfill your soul mission because that is what you were born to do. Taking the time to commune with your spirit guides means that you discover exactly what your mission is and receive guidance to fulfill *your* mission. The end result is that you feel far more satisfied with your efforts because you are achieving something that is genuinely meaningful *to you*.

Once you know what your mission is, and have confidence that you can achieve it, it becomes easier to set personal goals and pursue them because you have the innate, natural born motivation to fulfill those goals. The level of fulfillment you receive as a result is far deeper and more meaningful than any other level of fulfillment you may ever have the chance of experiencing.

Chapter 5: Defining the Terms of Your Relationship

For as long as you have been alive, you have been taught how to relate to other *humans*. You have discovered what social etiquette is, how to be proper in your relationships, and what is required of you in order for you to have a healthy relationship with the people around you. Spirit guides have not learned the same etiquette as you have, as they come from different realms that have different rules and etiquette for how to relate with others. While your spirit guides are not afraid of you and having relationships with you, you may be afraid of them and having relationships with them. After all, as humans, we are frequently told that the unseen is "wrong" or that people who talk about it are "strange." To our spirit guides, it's natural to relate to people across the realms.

In order to develop confidence in your relationships with your spirit guides, it can be helpful to know how to define the terms of your relationships and build your relationships in a way that feels good for you. Because your spirit guides only want what is best for you, they will happily oblige to any terms you set for your relationships as they want to help you communicate with them in a positive manner. Knowing that you define the terms of the relationship can make it much easier for you to develop confidence in your relationship with your spirit guides.

Developing a Relationship on Your Terms

Developing a relationship on your terms means deciding what type of relationship you want to have and how that relationship will feel. You get to decide when and how your spirit guides will connect with you, and what sort of boundaries you want to uphold. At first, it may seem like a good idea to let your spirit guides have "free range" to communicate with you anytime they want, but you must understand that spirit guides can be *eager*. They can connect with you in your waking and sleeping life to the point where you become overwhelmed by the communication. Some people even end up having to shut down the communication for a while because their own physical human energy becomes overwhelmed and challenging to navigate. In order to avoid this, you simply have to remember that *you get the final say*. That is the value of free will.

Before you ever communicate with your spirit guides, stop, and consider what would feel good and what would not feel good. As well, ensure that you remember that you always have the right to make adjustments to the terms as needed. For example, if you are fine with your guides communicating with you through clairvoyance most of the time but realize that it is overstimulating when you are driving, ask them to stop communicating when you are driving. In the very moment you ask, your terms will be respected, and the communication will stop. Your human energy may continue to feel interfered with for a short period of time, but there will be no additional interference affecting your energy field.

Using Free Will to Your Advantage

Using free will to your advantage in your relationship with your spirit guides is an excellent way to make sure that you are always in control. The way to use free will effectively is to remember that you have it in the first place and to assert your free will as needed. Never feel obligated to your spirit guides or allow yourself to hold the idea that you have to do anything, in particular, to be "eligible" for their support. The very fact that you exist and that they are a part of your spirit guide team means you are eligible, and they will be there to support you. While it is certainly ideal that you are kind and respectful to your guides and that you are considerate when talking to them, it is important to remember that the rules of human relationships are much different than the rules of spiritual relationships. This means if you do not want to follow your soul mission right now, but you do want to talk to your spirit guides, you can. Likewise, if you want to follow your soul mission but do not want any further relationship with your guides, you can do that, too. There is no right or wrong when it comes to upholding your relationships with your spirit guides.

Asserting Boundaries with Your Guides

Spirit guides will become rather pushy if you do not assert your boundaries because they do not realize they are being pushy. They will show up in your daydreams, in your dreams when you sleep, and in every single possible sign, symbol, and act of serendipity possible if you let them. Spirit guides love talking to you and showing their presence, and take great pleasure in communicating with you, so they will happily bombard your life with excessive communication if you let them. While it may seem like a fun idea, you still need to remain grounded and connected to human reality when communicating with your spirit guides. This means you need to have specific boundaries that you assert as needed to avoid your spirit guides accidentally disrupting your ability to stay grounded and focused on human reality.

When it comes time to assert your boundaries, you can assert them by giving your guides a clear rule. For example, "Do not communicate with me when I am at work, thank you." Or, "Do not communicate with me unless I specifically ask you to, or I am in serious danger and need assistance. Thank you." Asserting your boundaries in a loving manner helps you get your needs met, while still maintaining a positive relationship with your guides where the lines of communication remain open.

Chapter 6: Staying Protected During Communication

Even though you are going to be communicating with your guides, who are generally trustworthy and easy to work with, you must understand that upon opening the channels of communication, you are opening a channel to an alternate realm. Anytime you do this, there is the risk that other energies could come through, especially if you are unaware of what you are doing and how to adequately protect yourself from any energy you might encounter during your experience.

There are two simple rules to help you stay protected during the communication. The first is to know, with absolute certainty, that you are going to encounter other energies that want to penetrate your channel and find themselves in your energy field. The minute you start talking to your guides, these energies will see the channel and want to come in. Knowing this, you can be sure to take measures *every single time* to avoid letting unwanted energies come through.

The second rule is that you should never work with energy, or your guides before you know how to *stop*. This means if you are done communicating or want to close your channel, you know how to completely close it before you even open it in the first place. Knowing how to fully close and cleanse your channel, and yourself means you can protect yourself from having unwanted communications with anyone outside of yourself and your personal energy field. When you know with absolute certainty that something will try to come through and how to protect yourself from it happening, and you know how to close the channel anytime you need, you will be fully prepared to safely communicate with your guides.

Set Strong Intentions

One of the most powerful ways to work with the energy realms is to set strong intentions. To those who are unaware, an intention may seem like a mere idea of how they want things to go. This is a vague representation of what an intention is. Intentions are actually a way for you to decide on something, and then telepathically set the energy for said thing to occur within your energy field. For a practical example, consider the last time you set the intention to cook yourself dinner. It started with the idea that dinner needed to be cooked, then it manifested into the process of you making and eating the dinner. When you have strong intentions, you have the ability to completely shift your energy and gear it toward what you want, such as being protected from unwanted energy or enjoying a peaceful and positive communication with your guides.

To set an intention before any communication, you will simply close your eyes, set your intention, and hold that intention until you can physically feel it in all of your body and throughout your entire energy field.

If at any point during the session, you feel your energy straying away from the intention you had set, you can revisit the intention and allow yourself to reset that intention until you feel it within your entire being again. Then, when you are done, you can move back into your session. If you find that your energy is continually being violated or that it seems like you cannot maintain your intention, it may be best to end the session and try again later.

Learn to Differentiate Your Energy

When you work with spirits, whether it be to receive an energy healing session, to work with crystals, or to channel your spirit guides, there will always be other energies coming into your space. At times, it can be challenging to identify where your energy ends and the other energy begins. For example, if you are holding a crystal and it is infusing energy into your field, it may be challenging to identify what energy is yours that has been infused by the crystal, and what energy belongs only to the crystal.

Learning to differentiate your energy from the energy of anyone and anything else allows you to keep your energy pure and free of being infiltrated or overwhelmed by anyone else's energy. This way, you do not take on the energy, emotions, or experiences of anything else that is not intended to be experienced within your energy field.

There are four steps you can take to differentiate your energy from anyone else's energies. The first step is to notice any symptoms or experiences that seem to suddenly start around the same time your session starts, as this indicates that the energy you are experiencing is not your true energy. If you notice anything like this, dissociate from the unwelcomed energy and cleanse your own energy field as soon as possible.

The second step is to ask your intuition if you are experiencing your own energy or someone else's. Your intuition will usually respond with a "yes" or "no." If you feel "no" or any other signal indicating the energy you are experiencing is not your own, you can focus on removing that energy from your field through dissociating and cleansing.

The third step to differentiating between your energy and someone else's is to place a psychic energy shield around yourself and your energy field. Do this by visualizing a white light illuminating in the center of your body. Allow that light to grow and expand out, filtering out any energies that are not yours as it expands. If the energy is removed from your space during this process, you are experiencing someone else's energy.

The final step to differentiating is to spend a significant amount of time getting to know your own energy field and becoming familiar with your own energy, as well as the energy of any guides or tools you might be communicating with. This way, when you are working with your energy, you can clearly tell the difference between yours and the tools you are working with. You can also become familiar enough with your guides and tools that you can quickly tell when an unfamiliar and unwanted energy is presenting itself in your energy field.

Ground Your Energy Field Continually

It is a good idea to ground your energy routinely throughout the day, but there are times when you should engage in continuous grounding, too. When you are communicating with your guides or doing any sort of spiritual energy work, you should always be working toward grounding your energy. Grounding allows you to eliminate unwanted or excess energies back into the earth, completely eliminating them from your energy field. If you pick up any funky energies, or if your own energies start to become imbalanced in the process, the grounding practice will allow you to eliminate those energies and maintain your sovereign energy state.

There are two easy ways to ground, both of which can help you achieve this energy balance. The first involves your physical body and the earth; the second uses your breath to create the grounding effect. For the grounding practice that involves your physical body, you will keep your feet, or your tailbone pressed firmly into the ground beneath you. For the entire experience, you will visualize all of your unwanted, excess, or imbalanced energies being removed through your feet or tailbone into the earth below you. As you continue creating that connection, you will find your energies remain balanced, and you are less likely to experience any unwanted energies in your field.

If you want to use your breath to ground, you can practice maintaining a simple, rhythmic breathing pattern that allows you to control your energy field. As you breathe in, you visualize yourself receiving balancing energies that nourish your energy field and keep you grounded. As you exhale, you visualize any unwanted, excess, or imbalanced energies being released from your energy field so you can maintain your sovereign energy state. Some people will visualize the incoming energy as being white, yellow, or pink as they see this as being pure, clean energy that aids them in balancing and purifying their energy field. As they exhale, they visualize the outgoing energy as being black, indicating that they are releasing unwanted energy.

Use an Energetic Waterfall

Energetic waterfalls are a form of energy cleansing that can be used over an ongoing period of time. These do require your conscious awareness, though, so they are not necessarily something you can maintain for hours or days on end, but you can use them for the entire duration of a communication session or channeling experience. The purpose of the energetic waterfall is to have a waterfall that continually cleanses your energy field, washing away any unwanted energies as you go through your practice.

To create your energetic waterfall, you want to visualize white, yellow, pink, or light blue water-like energy pouring over you, exactly like a waterfall would. As you do, visualize it washing away any energy that does not belong to you, or that does not serve you. You can ask this same waterfall to completely cleanse your channel and the connection you have made to an alternate realm, too, to help you keep your connection clean and clear.

Anytime you find that your energy is being pressured or penetrated by unwanted energies, you can focus your attention on the waterfall for a few moments to visualize those energies being cleansed away. This combination of intention, the energy waterfall, and grounding will allow you to create a clean, safe space for you to communicate with your guides.

Enlist the Support of Crystals and Essential Oils

Practical protection tools like crystals and essential oils can be helpful when it comes to communicating with your guides. There are a variety of different crystals and essential oils that work, though it is best to stick to only using one or two of each to avoid overwhelming your energy system. While it might seem like having as many protective tools as possible would be ideal, it can actually be counterintuitive. Imagine going into battle, carrying far more shields than you could possibly need. It would take too much effort to carry the shields and attempt to use them, resulting in you being overwhelmed by the shields themselves, possibly leaving yourself open to attack. The same goes for practical spiritual tools.

If you want to enlist the support of crystals, reach for crystals like tiger iron, amethyst, fire agate, black tourmaline, tournalinated quartz, jet stone, black obsidian, smoky quartz, fluorite, or jasper. These crystals are all excellent for helping protect your energy physically, mentally, emotionally, and spiritually, so that you are not open to being attacked from energy on any plane, or in any way, whatsoever.

Essential oils can be used in several ways. You can use a single oil or a blend of oil. Many psychics create their own protection blends, which call on the use of many plant allies to help them create a strong protective field. You can diffuse the oil, anoint yourself with diluted oil, spray your room with the oil, or even use it as a body spray on yourself. The best essential oils for energy protection include lavender, lemon, cypress, grapefruit, frankincense, sage, and peppermint. You can also use sage incense or smudge sticks as a way to keep your space cleansed as you communicate with your guides, as both the sage itself as well as the smoke contain cleansing and protective properties.

End the Session If You Do Not Feel "Right"

Lastly, you need to have the confidence to follow your own intuition. If you are partaking in a session and communicating with your guides and find that something feels "off" or "not right," you need to trust that and assert your boundaries. Close the channel, cleanse your energy field, and ground to eliminate any unwanted energies from your space. It is important to understand that your guides will not be hurt, disappointed by, or upset with you for wanting to close the channel and communicate later. There is no reason to believe you are being rude, closing the channel for good, or somehow blocking off your guides by closing a channel prematurely. If things do not feel right, trust your intuition. You can always return to the channel to communicate with your guides again, later.

If you do find yourself having to close a channel because it feels "off," make sure you properly and thoroughly cleanse your energy and your space. Use incense or essential oil sprays, perform a crystal healing for yourself and your space (I teach you how in my book *Crystal Healing*), and use the power of intention and visualization to achieve your desired results. It is vital that you cleanse your energy and your space as soon as possible, as that "off" feeling you have could indicate that an unwanted energy has managed to cling to your energy or your space. A proper cleansing and grounding will eliminate the energy from that space so it cannot wreak havoc or lead to you struggling with your energy field. The longer you let an unwanted or negative energy cling to you or your space, the longer you will suffer from unwanted symptoms making it more challenging to eliminate that energy. Do not wait.

Chapter 7: Communicating with Your Guides

The process of actually communicating with your guides is far easier than you might think it is. There are many ways that you can invite your guides to come forth, communicate with you, and support you in whatever way you need them to. Over time, you will find a "signature communication style" that works best for yourself and your guides, consisting of your own "energy language," as well as your own methods for calling them forth and receiving guidance. Through this, you will come to recognize unique symbols and signs through which you can communicate. Until you reach that point, there are many wonderful beginner steps you can take to help you begin to communicate with your guides in a meaningful way. The more you communicate with your guides, the easier it will get, and the closer you will get to developing your own signature style.

Invite Them into Your Space

The first, and possibly most straightforward way of communicating with your guides is to invite them into your space. This part is truly as simple as closing your eyes, setting your intention, and inviting your guides to come forward to talk with you. You can invite your guides to help you with a specific purpose or, call them forward to share in casual conversation with you.

It is important to remember that you have free will, so unless you intentionally invite your guides into your space, they are unlikely to come forth. They might come forth in dire moments, but otherwise, they will stay away and wait for you to call. Anytime you find yourself stressed and begging "anyone" for help in your mind, have a near death experience or an intense life experience, or otherwise find yourself in a crazy situation, your guides will help you. Otherwise, they wait.

The flip side of free will is that if you invite your guides into your space and make it known that they can come in any time, *they will*. This can become overwhelming, so don't be afraid to ask them to give you space when it is needed, or to wait until they are called upon to begin communicating with you. Especially when you are new to communicating with your guides, having them openly coming into your space can be stressful.

Anytime you invite your guides into your space, it is still important to mind your intentions, cleanse your energy, and ground yourself. This may sound like a lot of work, but as you get used to communicating with your guides and using these energy techniques, you will find it becomes easier and easier for you to invite your guides into your space and maintain your energy.

Set a Special Space for Them

If you want to invite your guides in for a special experience, you might consider creating a special place for them. For intentional conversations or time spent together, it can be nice to play "host" or "hostess" to your guides by creating a wonderful atmosphere for you to share with your guides. Of course, this is not necessary, but it can be an empowering way to invite your guides into your space and have conversations with them as you get to know them and receive their guidance. Even those who have been talking to their guides for decades continue to this, as they feel that their guides are as close as their best friends or family.

As you set the atmosphere for your guides, consider what would feel nice and relaxing while also inviting. Light candles, burn incense, place some crystals around, brew a pot of tea, and create a comfortable environment for you to sit in. You can even get them a cup and make a place for them to sit if you would like. Some individuals with clairvoyant abilities can "see" their guides sitting across from them, so they do this as a way to communicate with their guides in a compassionate and welcoming way. Others do not "see" but instead simply feel the presence of their guides, so they are less worried about creating an official seat and more concerned with creating the right energetic environment to invite their guides into. You can set it up in whatever way feels right for you. Follow your intuition and, if you aren't sure, ask your guides how they would like your environment to be set up for special get togethers you might have with them.

Listen to Your Intuition

Your intuition is primarily your higher self speaking to you. Your higher self speaks to you with the intention of guiding you through life. From its higher vantage point, this part of you can foresee what choices are the best for you to make, how you should navigate different situations for the best outcome, and plenty of other information that you might not be privy to.

If you have yet to do any work with your third eye or are not particularly skilled with your clair senses, you can ask your guides questions and listen to your intuition to hear the answer. They will speak to you through that same gut feeling or gut voice that your higher self speaks to you through, offering as much guidance and insight as they possibly can into your unique situation.

If you are ever unsure about whether it is your intuition or your mind talking, give yourself the opportunity to pause and meditate first. Once you have meditated and quieted as many distractions as possible, it should be easier to hear your intuition and receive those messages. Your intuition is usually the first voice that pops up in your mind, or the automatic thought that follows the question or statement you have made in communicating with it. The more you develop trust in this, the easier it will be to communicate this way.

Talk Out Loud (Or in Your Mind)

Setting up a special atmosphere and getting everything ready for your guides is a wonderful way to share time with them, but it isn't the only way. Seasoned individuals who routinely talk to their guides often simply talk out loud, or in their minds, directing questions to their guides and receiving responses through their intuition and automatic thoughts. This is a perfect way of communicating with your guides, whether you have set out a specific space for them to join you, or you are wandering through your day to day life and are in need of guidance.

Often, the most obvious and straightforward ways of communication are the most powerful, yet as humans, we like to try to complicate things. It does not have to be complex; you can have these conversations as easily as you think thoughts to yourself.

Practice Intuitive Journaling

Intuitive journaling is a wonderful way to connect with your guides. Some people call this automatic writing, though it does not necessarily need to be automatic writing in order to be an experience where you communicate with your guides. Automatic writing is a practice where those who have activated their third eye allow another being to "take residence" in their body for a moment, essentially using their hand to write. This is a common way for mediums or psychics to contact deceased relatives or guides so they can receive messages through the form of writing. The individual rarely knows what is being said, so they have to read the message after it has been written to know what has come through.

When you use intuitive journaling, automatic writing can certainly be a practice you use to communicate with your guides. However, it is not the only way. You can also just ask questions and write down the first answers that come to your mind, or your intuitive answers, and keep track of them. As you engage in intuitive journaling with your guides, you are likely to become more confident in the messages you receive as you realize they have personalities and speak in nuanced ways that differ from your own. Further, you will likely start to see patterns in their messages, possibly leading to a greater understanding of what they are directing you towards.

Use Divinity Tools

Divinity tools are a great way to communicate with your guides. Tarot cards, oracle cards, scrying tools, and even crystal readings can be used as a way to communicate with your guides. When using these tools, it is important to understand that each one has its own set of rules, reading practices, and limitations. Always pick the tool that is right for the job and learn to interpret them appropriately. As well, be sure to continue your protection and grounding practices, as these tools also have the capacity to bring forth unwanted energies or entities since they are working within your channel. All of the same protection methods that you use for your intuitive channeling will work wonderfully for divinity tools, too.

Dreamwork and Visions

Dreamwork and visions are a powerful way of communicating with your guides. If you want to receive information from them but are looking for a more open experience, leverage the power of your dreams. During your dreams, you are relaxed and open, and you receive guidance from your guides with ease. Plus, dreamwork is surprisingly easy. The one drawback is that it can be easy to forget dreams, and they can sometimes be confusing. There are two steps to using dreamwork effectively.

The first step is to use the power of intention once again. Before you fall asleep, set the intention for what information you want to receive from your guides, and give them some advice on how they can communicate more clearly with you. This way, you have prepared yourself and them for the conversation, and you are more likely to receive the guidance you need from them. Once you have set your intention, release it, and focus on falling asleep. Your guides will show up to help answer your questions or provide you with whatever it is you have asked for. If they do not, try using a stone like amethyst, angel aura quartz, or Herkimer diamond under your pillow, as these all assist with lucid dreaming and dreamwork.

The second step is to keep a dream journal nearby. As soon as you wake up, write down everything you remember from your dream. At first, refrain from analyzing it as you may forget parts of it in the process. Write everything down, objectively, and from memory. Then, later, you can analyze what everything meant. An initial analysis can be done, but it is helpful to come back and analyze it again later so you can feel confident that you accurately interpreted the information from the dream.

Chapter 8: Talismans and Amulets for Your Guides

Talismans and amulets are a form of divinity tool that people have worked with for many centuries, across many cultures and religions. They are tools that are said to have magical powers that provide you with certain benefits, such as good luck or abundance. In the case of communicating with your guides, talismans and amulets can be used as a sort of "key" to your communication, helping you speak with your guides more clearly and effectively.

What Are Talismans and Amulets?

Talismans and amulets differ from each other, though many believe they are interchangeable. Talismans are generally something you wear, while amulets are something you hold or keep nearby. A talisman is usually something that has already been made, while amulets are something you can make for yourself.

Although talismans do not require you to make them yourself, they do still require effort on your behalf to ensure that they are ready for use. As with any new spiritual tool you bring into your life, you need to attune it to your energies and prepare it for the specific purpose you will be using it for. Often, the best way to know how to use a talisman is to follow your intuition. Some talismans may be passed down through families, in which case you may receive instruction on how to use that talisman to receive the full benefits of it.

Amulets do require you to make them, or for them to be made by someone else for you. It is not a good idea to buy an already-made amulet *unless* you feel your energy powerfully calling you toward it and essentially demanding you acquire said amulet. Otherwise, making your own amulet or having one intuitively made just for you is ideal, as this ensures that the amulet matches your energy. Rarely do you want to have a variety of amulets, as these are something that each person typically only has one or two of in their lifetime.

Finding Your Talisman

In some families, talismans are passed down as a tradition. As each new generation reaches a certain age, they are gifted the family talisman, and they are taught how to use it. These types of talismans generally have specific ways of being used, and they are best used in those specific ways. While you will cultivate your own relationship with the talisman and may incorporate your own nuances into how you use it, the general method will be the same between yourself and those before you.

If you do not have a family heirloom to use, you can still find and use a talisman. The key is to avoid looking for it. To truly find your talisman, ask your guides to direct you toward your talisman, and then stop looking. One day, as you are going about your everyday life, something will pop out at you, and you will know with absolute certainty from the depths of your existence that this is your talisman. It is essential that you listen to your intuition faithfully, as you do not want to jump on the first one you see out of excitement, only to find yourself doubting it later on. With the talisman that is truly meant for you, you will never doubt for a moment that it is the right one. Be patient until you find it.

Once you have found your talisman, you need to meditate with it. Ask it how it wants to be kept, used, and cared for. Give yourself time to get to know the talisman itself before using it for its intended purpose, as this ensures that you build a connection with it and are able to use it in a lasting, meaningful way. As you start to feel comfortable with it, use it for its intended purpose by bringing it into meditations, wearing it, or otherwise using it in any way it advised you to. The more you follow your intuition and the guidance of the talisman over the guidance of anyone else regarding how to use that talisman, the more powerful the talisman will be for you.

Making Your Own Amulet

Amulets are another divinity tool that may be passed down as family heirlooms. If you do not have an heirloom piece, though, you can create your own amulet. One way is to have someone intuitively design an amulet for you. If you truly object to your own creative abilities, there are many intuitives who can step forward to help you. These individuals will generally perform an energy reading on you, ask you why you want your amulet, and then intuitively create the amulet that they sense is meant for you. You can do your part by holding the intention of having exactly the right amulet, and by insisting your guides help in the process, so you receive exactly what you need and are looking for.

If you want to create the amulet yourself, the same level of intention is required. Stay intentional about the purpose of the amulet and request your guides to help you design it. Use anything you feel called to use, whether it be crystals, heirloom pendants or brooches, or other items. You can incorporate wire wrapping, clay sculpting, or even paper mâché into the process as you create the exact amulet that is meant for you. Let your creativity take you away, and by the end, you will have a beautiful amulet meant just for you and your guides.

After you have made your amulet, request that the amulet itself and your guides teach you how to keep, use, and care for the amulet properly. Follow your intuition to discover the true answers, as you want to keep this piece as personal as possible.

Using These Tools to Communicate

Once you have found your talisman or created your amulet, you need to be ready to use these tools to communicate. It is important that you understand that there are no hard and fast rules on how to use your talisman or amulet. In fact, the only rules you should truly be following are the ones your intuition and guides offer you, as this ensures that the communication experience remains personal and productive.

As a general rule of thumb to get you started, you can use these tools by wearing them or carrying them with you, or by meditating on them during specific communication sessions. This is a good way to get to know how to use it. From there, you may feel intuitively called to place it somewhere specific, wear it in a specific way, move it, or even hold it in your hand as you use it. Follow any and all guidance you receive, as this ensures that you are getting the most power out of it. Remember, when it comes to spiritual endeavors, nothing will come across to your guides as "silly" or "strange."

The same intuition will guide you when it comes to deciding where to store your talisman or amulet, how to store it, and how to take care of it. Again, follow this guidance. The more you can personalize this experience by trusting in your intuition over anything else, the more you will gain from this powerful tool.

Chapter 9: Thanking Your Spirit Guides

After you have communicated with your spirit guides, it is always nice to spend a few minutes saying thank you. Expressing gratitude is a wonderful way to keep positive, meaningful energy flowing back and forth between yourself and your guides. For your guides, receiving that gratitude makes them far more likely to work with you and follow your guidance as you educate them on how to best communicate with you. There are many ways you can express your thanks, though the following three ways are the easiest.

Offering Words of Thanks

The first and possibly easiest way of expressing gratitude to your guides is to simply say "thank you." Say thank you meaningfully and say it often. After you have intentionally carved out time for your guides, thank them for coming and express gratitude for any support or compassion they have offered during that time. If you are going about your day and receive sudden guidance that was much needed, express thanks. During casual conversations in your head, when you are driving home or doing something else, thank them for showing up and watching over you. When you experience a "miracle," a stroke of serendipity, or something positive, say thanks for any role they played in it. Frequently express your gratitude through words of thanks for the many ways they show up in your life, and they will graciously receive that gratitude from you.

Living Your Life with Gratitude

Your guides are often living alongside you in the life you are living, so a great way to express gratitude to them is to live your life with gratitude. What this means is that you express gratitude for everything, regardless of how it may or may not relate to them. As you go about your day, express gratitude for all the things you have and experience. When you are having a hard time, express gratitude for all of the positive things in your life. If you see a beautiful sunset, pet a cute animal, or have a nice time with a friend, express gratitude. Living your life in a state of gratitude means continually expressing thanks for the experiences they both directly and indirectly contribute to.

Gifts of Appreciation

Gifts of appreciation are always welcomed. For spirit guides, you might consider keeping a small bowl on your dresser and using it for your gifts of appreciation. In it, you can place small crystals, pieces of jewelry, or special treasures you found during your day, and other little gifts of appreciation. If you feel like it, you can even write them a letter and drop it into the bowl. Expressing appreciation through these little gifts is a wonderful way to offer thanks to your guides for everything they do for you.

Chapter 10: Getting the Most Out of Your Guides

If you really want to step up your experience and get the most out of your guides, it can help to truly understand just how much you can receive from these relationships. Advancing your relationships with your guides is like advancing your relationships with anyone else: the more you invest in and build upon the relationship, the more you can look forward to receiving from it. You might receive more frequent instances of guidance or clearer guidance, deeper feelings of support and love, greater joy derived from the relationship, or any other number of benefits. The key is to continually invest in advancing these relationships so that you can get more and more out of them.

Regularly Checking in With Your Guides

Perhaps one of the easiest ways to get the most out of your relationship with your guides is to regularly check in with them. Do not only check in when you need help, or sporadically when you feel like you have the time to sit down and engage in a longer conversation. At least weekly, but preferably several times a week, make time to talk with your guides. Check in with them through mental conversations when you are standing in a checkout line, ask them for help with a problem you are having at work or at home, or otherwise check in with them for little things. Even if you are dealing with something seemingly trivial, you can ask for help or chat with your guides and receive their support and love. The more you chat with your guides, the clearer your communication will become, and the more you will get from those relationships.

Having Casual Conversation with Guides

Not every conversation needs to be about your life going tragically wrong, or serious drama that is taking place in your world. Not everyone lives their lives with massive amounts of drama on an ongoing basis. Even if it seems like nothing is going on in your life or you have nothing to ask for, make time to talk to your guides. Regular, casual conversations help you connect with your guides in a positive, meaningful way. Ask them what their favorite way of giving signs is, then wait to see what sign you experience. Share with them about your day and listen to see if they have anything to say in return. When you see a sign that reminds you of your guides, let them know you are thinking about them and offer words of admiration or appreciation. These casual conversations are wonderful for building up your relationships with your guides and creating strong, lasting bonds with them.

Learning Their Unique Energy and Personality

Every guide has its own unique energy and personality. Spending time getting to know the energy and personality of your guides is a wonderful way to become familiar with who they are and what presence they are likely to bring forth in your life. The more you get to know their unique energy, the more comfortable you will feel around them.

The easiest way to understand the benefit of this is to think about your friends. Before you knew them, your friends had foreign personalities and energies that were entirely unfamiliar to you. Because of that, they might have been somewhat uncomfortable to be around because you did not know who they were or what to expect. You might have been careful with the words you used, only exposed certain parts of yourself, and held things back to avoid offering parts of yourself that may have been judged by that person. This is natural when we do not know the person we are communicating with. Once you got to know your friends, you came to understand their unique energy and personality, and you felt far more comfortable and confident enjoying a relationship with them. You stopped worrying about what to say or how to act and started feeling certain in the way you could behave in that relationship. The same goes for your relationship with your guides. As you come to understand who they are, you begin to understand how you can engage with them, and your relationships grow stronger as a result.

Calling on Your Guides Anytime You Need Help

If you are not used to communicating with your guides, it may seem unnatural to call on them when you need their help. Rather than feeling supported and like you have someone you can call on anytime you need them, you might instead feel like you have to face everything alone. As you grow used to having your guides around, it helps to start asking them for help more often. You can never ask for "too much" help, as they are in your life for the sole purpose of helping you. Ask them for help as often as you need, no matter how big or small your situation might be. The more you ask, the more help you will receive, and the more value you will gain from these relationships.

Following the Guidance You Are Offered

When you are offered guidance from your guides, it helps to actually take that guidance. This will benefit your relationships in three ways and will maximize the value you gain from your guides massively. First, following their guidance shows your guides that you trust them and that you willingly receive their guidance and support. This will likely make them begin to show support even more abundantly.
Second, you learn to trust in them and the guidance they offer, and it becomes easier for you to feel confident that the messages they are sending are truly coming from them and not from some foreign voice inside of yourself.

Third, when you follow the guidance of your guides, you receive the results you desire. This guidance is tailored to help you manifest anything and everything you want, so as long as you follow it, you will always arrive at your desired outcomes. It's a no-brainer to follow it as often, and as closely, as you can!

Having Back and Forth Conversations

It can feel strange and uncomfortable to routinely communicate with someone, only to feel as though they are not communicating back with you. If you do not feel automatic thoughts or "intuitive messages," coming through from your guides, learn to have back and forth conversations in other ways. Ask them a question about themselves and then direct them to a sign they can offer you to signify the answer. For example, you might say, "Are you with me right now? Show me a pink flower if you are." Then, a pink flower might blow across your path. You can practice engaging in a variety of different back and forth conversation styles with your guides through trial and error. As you do, you will discover that there really is someone or something right there listening and communicating back with you, making it easier to feel confident in your communications with them in the first place. This way, you stop wondering if someone is listening, and instead, you know from the bottom of your heart that someone truly is there watching over you.

Conclusion

Congratulations on completing *Spirit Guides!*

This book was written to help you understand who your spirit guides are, why they exist, and how you can begin to rely on them for greater support in your life. Your spirit guides are powerful beings who exist to help you in life, in any way you desire. The more you learn to work with your guides and rely on them, the stronger your senses will become, and the more powerful their guidance will be for you.

I hope that through reading this book, you realize that you are abundantly supported and that you stand to gain so much from life. With the support of your guides, there is nothing you can't do. Whether you want to manifest greater happiness and deeper joy from life, a penthouse or beautiful house on the lake, financial security, or anything else, it can all be achieved through knowing your guides and feeling comfortable asking them for help. As you ask your guides for help, you can rely on them to point you in the right direction and support you with becoming the most powerful version of yourself possible. Before you know it, you will be manifesting everything with ease through the help of your guides.

Now that you have reached the end of this book, I encourage you to think long and deep about the value of your spirit guides. If you are ready, spend time in meditation talking to them and getting to know who they are and what they have to offer you. Learn to express gratitude, communicate with them freely, and receive signs from them. If you have nothing to ask for yet, or if you are not yet sure of how to receive their messages, ask them for signs and then look for those signs that they offer. Always remember, the more effort you put into your relationships with your guides, the more you will get out of them.

Finally, I'd like to thank you for taking the time to read this book. I hope you have found it to be both interesting and informative, and I wish you the best of luck in your spiritual endeavors!

www.ingramcontent.com/pod-product-compliance
Lightning Source LLC
LaVergne TN
LVHW021735060526
838200LV00052B/3292